BRITAIN IN OLD PHOTOGRAPHS

LEICESTER
AT WORK

DAVID R. BURTON

ALAN SUTTON PUBLISHING LIMITED

Alan Sutton Publishing Limited
Phoenix Mill · Far Thrupp · Stroud
Gloucestershire · GL5 2BU

First published 1995

Copyright © David R. Burton

Cover photographs: front: Granby Street,
1903–4. *Back*: W. Bennett, Humberstone Gate,
1896. *Title page*: Milkman Sidney Hitchens,
1927.

British Library Cataloguing in Publication Data.
A catalogue record for this book is available from
the British Library.

ISBN 0–7509–1031–3

Typeset in 9/10 Sabon.
Typesetting and origination by
Alan Sutton Publishing Limited.
Printed in Great Britain by
Ebenezer Baylis, Worcester.

This book is dedicated to my grandchildren, Matthew,
Joseph, Sarah, Emma and Benjamin for all the joy
they bring to my wife Beryl and myself.

The fate of the 100-year-old Britannia Statue hung in the balance when the Granby Street Britannia works were scheduled for demolition. The corporation preserved the statue, which is shown here in 1965.

Contents

Granby Street, 1903–4. The trenches in the photograph were part of the transport department's work in preparation for the change to electric trams. On the left is Chatham Street and the Grand Hotel.

Introduction

In 1993 *Leicester in Old Photographs*, my first book, was published. A second selection followed in 1994 and now book number three, *Leicester at Work*.

I have been overwhelmed by the reaction to the first two volumes, both sold out in a very short time. Letters have poured in, mostly of thanks for jogging memories of years gone by, as well as letters and phone calls from past school friends, work colleagues and former neighbours.

The photographs in this book are mostly from the archives of the *Leicester Mercury* and so the quality is first class. I have uncovered a photograph of Mr K.K. Knight, the men's outfitter, whose three shops were situated under the Grand Hotel in Granby Street. I worked there in 1956 with George Moore, who was manager of the shirt shop, Peter Bull and Roy Finn. Situated as it was under the hotel, the shop had many famous customers like Bill Maynard, Jimmy James, Clement Atlee and many more.

The memory is a wonderful thing, and I trust that these old photographs will jog it to recall events, some good, some bad, some happy, some sad and some we would sooner forget, but mostly events from days gone by which will give pleasure in some form or another. I hope you enjoy my book, and the memories of factories, shops and the friends you knew when you were at work.

David R. Burton.

Stead and Simpson Ltd at 12 Belgrave Gate just before their move to a new warehouse at Syston. The firm had been at Belgrave Gate since 1860. The building is no longer there.

London Road station, 1 October 1962: no trains today. Secretary of the Leicester No. 1 National Union of Railwaymen branch in Leicester at the time was Mr Jack Worley.

TRANSPORT

A tram with decorations to mark the homecoming of Leicester soldiers, c. 1918.

One of the last horse-drawn trams climbing London Road on its way to Melbourne Hall, *c.* 1904. A third horse was added to help with the hill.

Tramcar No. 144 at the Abbey Park Road depot, 1914. It was used on the Narborough Road route from March 1913, and was designed with large platforms so that passengers could pay for their fares as they boarded.

A sorry sight for tram lovers, *c*. 1980. This is No. 59, which once rattled its way to Aylestone and Belgrave from Stoneygate to Humberstone. The tram was discovered in a field in Markfield.

A familiar sight in *c*. 1960, a corporation bus, but this one is unusual. It is an AEC Renown with double rear axles.

A Co-operative milkman at work, *c.* 1950. It is believed to be Sidney Hitchens. This photograph brings back memories for the author, who was a Saturday boy with Freeman Moulton of Barclay Street. The milkround was in the Barkby Road area in the 1950s.

A pre-1920 Premier motor cycle, single cylinder, belt drive, acetylene headlamp, and a Leicester registration.

Mr Fred Loones, a coal merchant of Humberstone Road wharf, *c.* 1930. On the cart is a large lump of coal and the public were invited to guess the weight at *6d* a go. I wonder what the prize was?

Another milkman, 1916. Unfortunately his name is not known.

A coach party outside the Three Crowns on the corner of Horsefair Street and Granby Street, c. 1865. The Three Crowns was one of Leicester's most important coaching inns. It was built in 1726 and demolished in 1869 to make way for the National Provincial Bank (now National Westminster).

An outing for the staff of Poole Lorrimer and Tabberer of King Street, c. 1900. The scene is at Thurmaston Lane bridge.

The Lord Mayor and Lady Mayoress, Sir Mark and Lady Henig, unveiling the plaque to commemorate the improvement of the Lime Kiln Lock, near Abbey Park Road, for the National Rally of Boats, July 1967.

Narrow boats at the Belgrave Road wharf, 1956. The cargo of steel coils is bound for London and then Spain.

Mr Reg Barnett at work on a British Waterways dredger on part of the Grand Union Canal on the outskirts of Leicester, *c.* 1980.

An accident on the railway bridge over the main Uppingham Road, *c.* 1968. The bridge was taken away following the closure of the Old Great Northern Railway line.

All trains in and out of Leicester were halted for an hour after five ballast wagons were derailed at a bridge above Ulverscroft Road in 1992.

An ASLEF meeting in the Trades Hall, 8 June 1955. On the front row is Mrs G. Swann, wife of the Branch Secretary, and Mrs H. Wood, an engine driver's wife.

A fatal rail accident near Leicester, 7 September 1972. Rescue workers are trying to reach the trapped crew. The driver, Mr Wally Horne, was released after four hours. Unfortunately Mr Michael Denman, the crewman, did not survive.

A rail accident, 1912. The site is believed to be north of the Midland station at the Vulcan Road bridge.

Section Two

EDUCATION

Abbey Park Road School, Leicester, c. 1902. The teacher is Miss Sarson and the headmaster Mr Read.

Pupils of the Greencoat School, *c.* 1873. In 1762 Alderman Gabriel Newton, who lived in Highcross Street, left £3000 to the corporation to found a school for boys whose parents were members of the Church of England. It was called the Greencoat School and was in the Shambles near St Nicholas Church.

Moat Road School, Standard Seven, 1905.

Bridge Road School, 1907. The teacher is Miss Kelly, the headmaster at the time was Mr Badderly. Far right second row is Ron Banner. Starched collars were a must for important occasions.

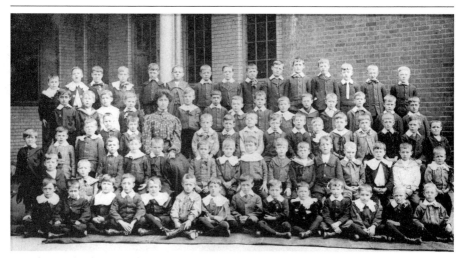

Mantle Road School, probably in 1906. The teacher is Miss Percy.

Bridge Road Junior School, c. 1909. Mr J. Driver is the teacher and included in the photograph are Earnest Wynne (bottom left) and Bill Heywood (third from right, back row). Bill Heywood became Leicester's first police motor cyclist.

Medway School Infants class, 1906. Starched collars for the boys and lace for the girls were the order of the day.

King Richards Road School Choir, *c.* 1900. Only part of the photograph is shown as it is very faded. Mr Cooper was headmaster at the time and Mr Vile the choirmaster.

Pupils from Moat Boys' School touring the *Leicester Mercury* headquarters in St George Street, March 1978. Mr David Illson, the photographic printer, is explaining the process.

THE LEICESTER
MERCURY

A typical Leicester Mercury *front page,*

16 December 1966.

An aerial view of the site for the new *Mercury* offices, taken from Holy Trinity spire, 1963.

Mr A.W. Peake, Chairman and Managing Director of the *Leicester Mercury*, Mr Malcolm McAlpine of Sir Robert McAlpine and Sons Limited and Mr J.M. Hepburn at the topping out ceremony at the new St George Street headquarters of the *Leicester Mercury, c.* 1965.

The final lap, *c.* 1990. The newsvendor, out in all weathers, a cheerful friend of the public.

Leicester Lord Mayor Councillor Peter Kimberlin and Lady Mayoress Mrs Doreen Kimberlin get to grips with technology at a visit to the *Mercury* offices, 17 May 1990. Also pictured are Mr Hollingworth and Joanne Durham.

The *Leicester Mercury* composing room, 1972.

The *Leicester Mercury* print room, 3 December 1986. Photographed are Mr John
P. Aldridge, Chairman and Managing Director, with Mr Ralph Price.

One of the giant printing machines at the *Leicester Mercury*, 3 February 1967.

A large machine on the move at the *Mercury* in Albion Street, 1967.

Local newsagents touring the *Leicester Mercury* headquarters in St George Street, 1982. They are in the wire (telegraph) room with Mr Robert Hughes, a member of staff.

Moving day. The *Mercury* moves to its new St George Street premises, 1967.

Section Four

SERVICES

Leicester Fire Brigade outside the fire station, c. 1900.

Leicester fire station in Lancaster Road, 1954.

Firefighters in Leicester with one of the first motorized fire engines acquired by the Leicester Fire Brigade, c. 1900.

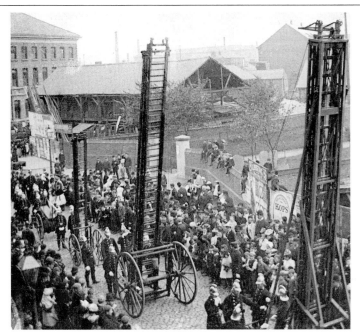

Leicester Fire Brigade on parade in Rutland Street, 1892.

A Leicester Fire Brigade horse-drawn escape outside the Asfordby Street fire station, 1899. The horse's name is Charlie.

Leicester Fire Brigade, Asfordby Street, 1905. Mr Fred Ames is pictured top row far right.

Emergency, *c.* 1959! When this furniture van caught fire, the driver was directed to the fire station where the blaze was put out.

An exercise at the passing-out parade at Leicester fire station, 1955. The 'victim' is being given a fireman's lift down the ladder.

A men's Sunday school, 1898. Mr William Ely, a superintendent in the Leicester Fire Brigade, was superintendent of the Sunday school. His two sons are pictured: back row first left is Tom, with Albert fourth from the left. Mr Tom Beardsmore is standing next to Albert and far right on the back row is Mr E.H. Lord.

The fire station alarm control room, 1958. There were eighty-eight premises with direct links to the station. Fireman Spence is checking the board.

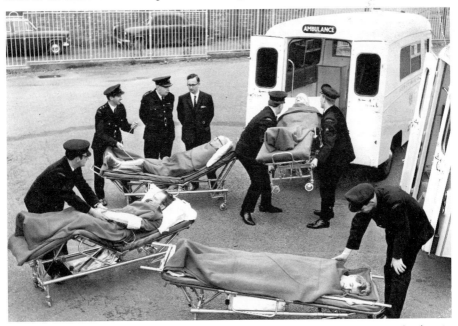

Leicester ambulance service, 1968. Leicester ambulance service was among the first in the country to be equipped with removable trolley beds. The beds could be used in six different positions.

The engineering staff of the Leicester Corporation Gas and Electric Lighting Department, 1899. Back row, left to right: H. Bourne, D.F. Colson, T. Roles, L. Trewby, A. Charlton, V.E. Wakerley, G. Charlton, H.E. Clayton. Front row: W.E. Barton, J.E.M. Stewart, A. Colson (engineer), E.W. Frost, J.T. Blake.

The city ambulance service, outside Prebend House, 1945.

Leicester conductors and conductresses outside the Abbey Park Road tram depot during the First World War.

Mr Bill Ryland, Chairman of the Post Office Board, has a word with switchboard operator Tina Sandbrook in the new Charles Street offices, 1971.

The Post Master General Mr E. Short talking with operatives in the Leicester telegraph department, 1967. Left to right: Mrs R. Walters, Mr E. Short, Mr J. Williams, Mr R. Harper, Mrs T. Jesson.

The newly opened Stocking Farm post office, 1956. Pictured in the busy office are Mrs S. Matlock, Mrs D. Rylett and Mrs D.M. Fazackerley.

Sir Barnet Janner MP opening the new sub-post office at Mowmacre, 1964. The office was part of the Leicester Co-operative society's branch. Mr F. Gray, the manager, is in the white coat.

The Royal Tigers Association members in Town Hall Square after their annual parade service at the cathedral, 24 June 1974.

The Tigers company, led by Major Anthony Swallow, at the march past in Victoria Park. The salute was taken by the Lord Mayor, Mrs Irene Pollard.

Section Five

ENGINEERING – MANUFACTURING

Francis Theodore Wain and his wife Ellen outside

their home, 24 Langton Street, off Belgrave Gate,

c. 1927. The sign reads Timber Merchants.

The Wallace and Wright Engineering Works in Great Holme Street, 1939.

Wallace and Wright employees at work in their factory, 1939.

A general view of the mill at the woodworking factory of John Mason and Sons of Nottingham Road, St Saviours, Leicester, *c*. 1900.

William Gimson's new premises in Upperton Road, 1959. The Swan Island site, covering 22 acres, is being developed. The site is bounded by the canal and the River Soar. The main central Leicester–London railway and the Midland Leicester–Burton line can be seen.

A fine aerial photograph of William Gimson's premises at Swan Lake Mill, Upperton Road, Swan Island, 1990. On the right at the top is Filbert Street, the Leicester City Football Club ground.

Mr Stan Calow and Mr Bill Thacker of William Gimson and Sons push a trolley containing Keroing from Malaya and Utile from West Africa into a kiln for drying, 1967. To dry completely it takes three weeks in the kiln but twelve months in normal weather conditions.

Mr Tony Ross operates a machine which makes up roof trusses in a matter of minutes at William Gimson and Sons, 1967.

One of the many powerful saws which William Gimson and Sons have in their mill, 1967.

The manufacture of prefabricated roof trusses, 1967. These were introduced for the first time in Leicester by William Gimson and Sons.

An old Bedford lorry and a Ruston excavator belonging to the Jelson building firm, 1950. Here they are removing clay from the Clarendon Engineering site. The Jelson story started in 1889 when James Jelley started as a self-employed joiner and shopfitter from his home in Shenton Street. By the 1930s a semi-detached house cost £650; by 1967 the cost had risen to £1,770.

A Parker mobile primary and secondary crusher, c. 1980. The crusher produced four different sizes of road stone at a time.

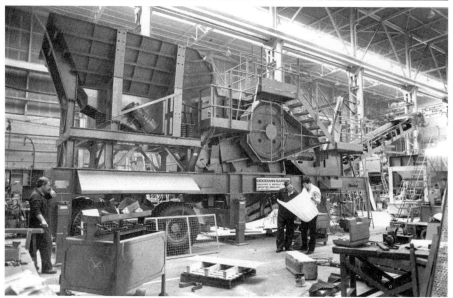

Dwarfed by a giant crusher at Goodwin Barsby are Mr Mick King (left) and Mr Richard Pegg, works manager, *c.* 1980.

Mr David Auty (centre), Managing Director of Goodwin Barsby, with Mr Norman Thorold (right) and Mr Bill Petitt (left), both long-serving members of the company, *c.* 1980. In the background is a Goodwin Goliath crushing plant. The author worked a 30 × 18 crusher for Crushstone Quarries at Woolfox quarry near Stamford, Lincolnshire, in the 1960s.

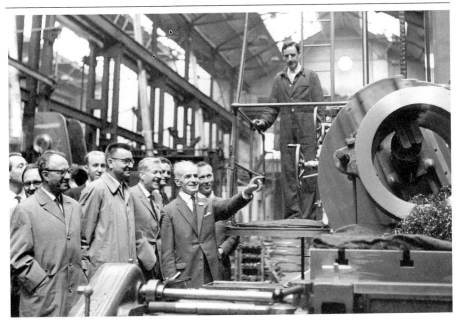

Mr Freddy Preston, works director of Goodwin Barsby and Company Limited, showing visitors from overseas around the Leicester works, 1963.

An open day at Parker Plant to mark 80 years of manufacturing at their Canon Street, Belgrave works, c. 1990. The large machine is an 1180 Jan Crusher for crushing stone.

A trio from Parker Plant, 1979. Left to right: Mr Bill Abbott, Mr Ken Parker and Mr Ken Holmes. The men were due to go to Buckingham Palace as representatives of companies who had won the Queens Award to Industry.

A section of the machine shop at the works of Frederick Parker Limited, *c.* 1980. The machines are tape-fed Batchmatics.

A dry mix concrete plant made by Frederick Parker Limited for the Cliff Hill Granite Company, although it was never used by them. Ready Mixed Concrete (Leicester) Limited acquired the machine some two years later. The photograph was taken in 1961.

Her Royal Highness The Duchess of Kent talking to Frederick Pollard and Company Limited director Mr Bill Spencer-Brown and Mr Brian Pollard, 1975. With the Duchess is Mr Bill Pearce of the British Overseas Trade Board.

The fitting shop of Frederick Pollard and Company Limited at the 'Corona' machine tool works, 1938.

The machine shop at Frederick Pollard, St Saviours Road East, Leicester, 1938.

Frederick Pollard and Company Limited, 1968. In the turning shop are, left to right: Mr A. Brown, shop foreman, Mr T. Ball and Mr J. Reid.

The Frederick Parker 75th Anniversary dinner dance, 1987. Left to right: Mr Raymond Pollard, Mr Ted Smith, who had served 50 years with the company, Mrs Gertrude Pollard, Mr Fred Wade (50 years), Mr Jack Caple (52 years), Mr Ken Hudson (54 years) and Mr Brian Pollard, Managing Director.

A Stibbe knitting machine, 1968. The firm was among the top four knitting machine manufacturers in the world. This machine is being tested by Mr Frank Scroby with 45 years in the trade.

The Metal Box Company of Leicester, 1967. Mr Norman Hartley watches waste metal being automatically ejected after lids have been cut out.

In 1968, within the works of the Leicester Carriage Builders, vehicles are prepared for Japan, America, Holland and Zambia as well as the home market.

The foreman of Leicester Carriage Builders workshop and Mr Tom Knight, an inspector, discuss a problem in the paint shop, 1968.

The outside of the Gent and Company factory in St Saviours Road, Leicester, *c.* 1960.

Members of staff at Jones and Shipman, *c.* 1980. Left to right: Mr Tom Mee, design engineer, Mr Charlie Gell, fitter, Mr Bob Reed, inspector, and Mr Brian Hollingsworth, chief inspector.

Her Royal Highness Queen Elizabeth asked to see a working factory during her visit to Leicester in 1980. She is pictured here with Mabel Hardy and directors of Jones and Shipman.

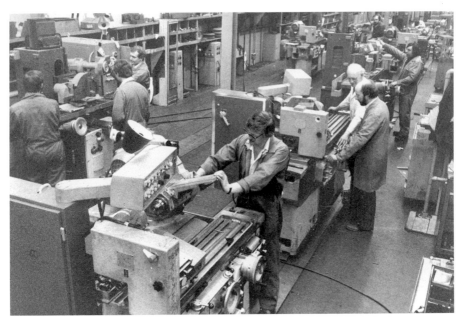

The fitting shop at Jones and Shipman, 1980.

Dunlop Rubber, St Marys Mills. Mr A. Robinson checks the specification of white tyrewall rubber. Dunlop took over the factory from W. and A. Bates in 1925.

A new machine at Imperial Typewriters of Leicester, *c*. 1961. It consisted of three typewriters joined together with exchangeable carriages in different languages.

THE HOSIERY TRADE

A fine view of H.T.H. Peck Ltd, manufacturerers of Pex socks and stockings, 1987. On the left is the Kirby & West Dairy.

A scene of peace and tranquillity along the canal from West Bridge, 1990.

Mr S. Wade, Mr Michael Kissane and Mr Ron Spence at H.T.H. Peck Ltd, 1967.

Mr Peter Bailey of H.T.H. Peck Ltd (far right) with, left to right, Mr Colin Harris, Miss Evelyn Rimmington, Mr Cyril Cockbill, Mrs Mary Knight, 1975.

Mr Peter Bailey, Chairman and Managing Director of H.T.H. Peck Ltd, with members of the Quarter Century and Forty Year clubs, 1979. Left to right: Miss Jean Gillett, Mr Alan Hankin, Mrs Joan Kidd, Mr Denis Louch and Mrs Nora Gilliver.

Mr Bernard Garfoot operating a Bentley Komets machine at the West Bridge factory of H.T.H. Peck Ltd, 1977.

Pictured at H.T.H. Peck Ltd are, from the left, Mrs Elsie Fray, Miss Valerie Massey and Mrs Louise Hill, 1967. The ladies are examining, folding and boxing tights.

Managing Director Mr Peter Baily of H.T.H. Peck Ltd, with a zodiac machine which he won in a raffle, 1967. The machine was made in Italy.

Pex socks and stockings, 1983. The factory steams away while the canal is dark and calm.

Byfords Hosiery and Knitwear factory in Abbey Lane, *c.* 1980. The company began in Bedford Street in December 1919 and by 1969 employed nearly 2,000 people.

Mrs Hazel Wade tests sock strength in the examining section at D. Byford & Co. Ltd, 1968.

A director of D. Byford & Co. Ltd (left) presenting socks and sweaters to Lieutenant Commander Alexander Sinclair RN, Secretary of the British Schools Exploring Society, 1969. The garments are to be worn on an expedition to Newfoundland.

Mr Donald Byford, Chairman, and Mrs Byford (right) welcome Colonel R.A. St G. Martin, Lord Lieutenant of Leicestershire, and Mrs Martin at the firm's Golden Jubilee dinner in 1969.

The Golden Jubilee dinner at D. Byford & Co. Ltd. Left to right: Mr A.V. Parker (Managing Director), the Right Honorable Viscount Watkinson, Mrs A.V. Parker, Mr C. Barrie Byford and Mr John Wegerif, Managing Director of the Bentley Group.

Major General Sir Jeremy Moore (on the right) inspects a garment with Mr Nicholas Corah (left), Chairman of Corahs, 1985. Centre is Mr Bill Simpson.

Dalma works in Junior Street, acquired by N. Corah (St Margarets) Ltd, 1960.

Some members of the staff of N. Corah & Sons St Margarets works, who have been with the firm for a period of between 25 and 56 years. The year is 1912.

Sir John Corah, former chairman of N. Corah (St Margarets) Ltd, joins workmen in a celebration drink after laying the foundation stone of the company's new £350,000 factory which was being built in St John Street, Leicester, 1964.

Yvonne Spencer, a 15 year old in her third week in the Corah training school, receives instruction from Mrs Dorothy Beck, 1969.

Mr C. Hubbard (in shirt sleeves) of R. Rowley & Co. Ltd, chargehand of the test shop, examines material from a patternlock machine, 1968. With Mr Hubbard is Mr W.A. Gamble, production director.

Ravens hosiery factory in Wharf Street, *c.* 1920. A very industrious scene.

The materials inspection department at Richard Roberts Knitwear Ltd of Vaughan Way, 1968.

The staff in the hosiery department at Frisby Jarvis & Co. Ltd, 1967.

Mr Brian Lodge (centre), Chairman and Managing Director of Toller and Lankester of Grace Road, with members of staff, 1987. I was privileged to live next door to Mr Harold Thornley, a director of the company, who was known to my brother and myself as 'Pal', which he was.

Taylors factory in Havelock Street, due to close in 1958.

Section Seven

BOOTS AND SHOES

Mr Charles Clore presents a pair of silver candelabra to the Lord Mayor of Leicester,

Alderman Harold Heard, and Lady Mayoress, Mrs Heard, for the civic plate collection on

behalf of Freeman Hardy and Willis, the Leicester shoe manufacturers, July 1962. Many

West End people will remember Alderman Heard as their Hinckley Road butcher.

Mr Ian Oliver of Olivers Shoes with his wife Janet and the Duke of Rutland, *c*. 1971. They are pictured at the official opening of the new factory at Castle Acres, Narborough. The author's late father-in-law worked for Olivers for nearly 50 years.

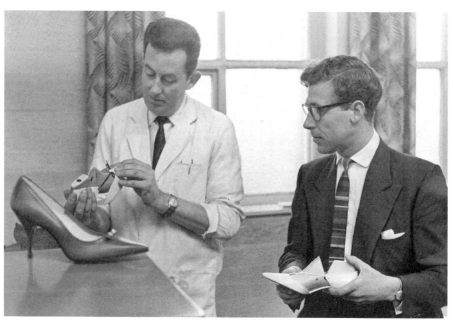

Peter Marshall and Douglas Greenway discuss what the ladies will wear in 1963 at the Co-operatives Wheatsheaf Leicester factory.

Three employees of the British United factory, *c*. 1980. Left to right: Mr Arthur Jarman, Mr Fred Simmons, Mr Demetrio Sposato. They have one hundred and thirty years service between them.

British United Shoe Machinery Limited, *c*. 1980. On the right is Mr Ken Birch, the sheet metal section manager, and Mr Graham Gregg, foreman. The machine is a Trumpf C.N.C. punch press.

G.U.S. Footwear Ltd of Melton Road. Pictured here in 1968 are 23-year-old Colin Powell, 4 ft 6 in, and 46-year-old Peter Wright, 6 ft 3 in.

Members of staff in the sample department at G.U.S. Footwear Ltd, 1968. Left to right: Mrs Freda Agar, Mrs Nellie Penrose, Mrs Evelyn Smith and Mrs Kath Steel.

Mrs Ivy Stuart had worked for F.J. Palfreymans Shoes for 35 years when this photograph was taken in 1968.

Mr Sid Jones of F.J. Palfreymans, an expert press clicker, 1968. The company was founded in 1907.

Portland Shoes factory on the corner of Newarke Close, 1988. The manufacture of boots and shoes was one of Leicester's finest industries.

Portland Shoes; hand craftmanship is still very evident in this photograph taken *c*. 1970. The craftsmen are Mr Louis McKey and Mr Sydney Lay with Mr Malcolm Usher, sales director, looking on.

Mr George Hurst, heeling in the press room at Smith Faire & Co. Ltd, 1968.

Left to right: Mr Derek Purnell, Managing Director of Portland Shoes, Mr Roy Astrop, design director, and Mr Malcolm Usher, commercial director, 1984.

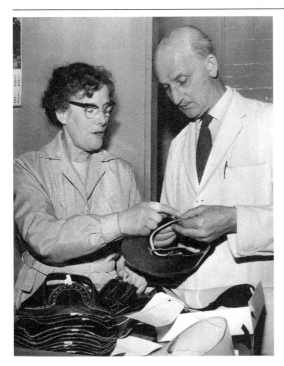

Mrs Vera Macbean and Mr Harold Bradley of Smith Faire & Co. Ltd, boot and shoe manufacturers of St Saviours Road, Park Vale works, 1968. At this time the company employed 200 staff; it closed in 1982.

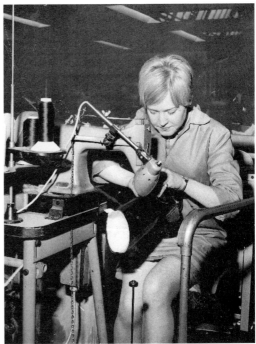

Jean Briggs, a back seaming machinist at Smith Faire & Co. Ltd, is stitching a boot back seam, 1968.

J. W. LE-BUTT,
Boot Maker & Repairer,
62, WELFORD ROAD, LEICESTER.
Repairs sent for and returned to any address.

J.W. Le Butt, a boot and shoe maker and repairer in Welford Road, 1927.

No. 141 Belgrave Road, a small shop that sold everything, c. 1915. Miss Nellie Wayte, the manageress, is standing in the doorway.

Section Eight

FOOD AND DRINK

The Fox's Glacier Mint factory in York Road, 1969. Mr W.R. Fox founded a wholesale grocery and confectionery company in Leicester in 1894. Mr Eric Fox, his son, developed the popular mint flavour and his two sons, Bruce and Ian, kept the ingredients secret until the company merged with John Mackintosh and Sons Limited in 1969.

Mrs B. Howlett collects fresh biscuits and sends them on to the next process at Nabisco Frears, 1967. Frears was established in 1926.

Mr M. Joyce checks biscuits at Nabisco Frears as they pass along the conveyor, 1967.

The flour store room at Squires and Kintons in Humberstone Lane, 1954. Here the flour is sieved and then piped to the mixers as it is needed.

The dough-making machine at Squires and Kintons, 1967. Far removed from the village baker the author knew as a lad.

David Chapman and David Buckley making Danish pastries at Squires and Kintons, 1967.

Squires and Kintons, 1967. David Chapman operates the automatic pastry roller.

The bread slicer at work at Squires and Kintons, 1967.

Walkers Crisps in Barkby Road, 1967. Mrs Beryl Weirson sorts through reject packets of crisps.

Walkers Crisps, 1967. Mrs Sheila Crane packs another load for despatch. They are sent from Leicester all over the country.

Walkers Crisps, 1967. Mr Alan Lawrence at the console of machinery which automates the process of crisp manufacture.

Not a pub crawl but a publicans' steam, 1988. Licensees from Everards Brewery joined Mr Richard Everard (far right), the company chairman, for a trip on a steam train. Also present from Leicester are David and Marabelle Munday (Saracens Head), Kevin and Andrea Wragg (Old Robin Hood), Martin and Lesley Webster (Victory), Bob and Jessie Main (The Dove) and Ronald and Geraldine Bentley (Bridge Lane Tavern).

Everards Brewery in Castle Street,
Leicester, 1937.

Kirby and West automatic filling and capping, 1968.

The Kirby and West Dairy Company was started in 1868.

The milkman at work at the corner of Newmarket Street and Gilliver Street, Knighton, c. 1930. The art of ladling the milk from churn to jug was quite a skill.

The Porters Arms at 36 East Bond Street was kept by Anne L. Jones. The public house was aptly named as the large building in the background eventually became Bond Street Nursing Home and Maternity Hospital, where the porters' residence was also situated. At the time of the photograph it was of course Fielding and Johnson's factory in West Bond Street. The breeches shop next door to the pub is William Stewart's. Today the whole site is part of the Shires shopping complex.

The Horn of Plenty, *c.* 1900. What a grand name for a little pub tucked away in Lower Garden Street off Belgrave Gate. Samuel Sibson was the proprietor in 1902.

The Three Cranes at the corner of Humberstone Gate and Wharf Street, *c.* 1911. It was the headquarters of the Leicester Bicycle Club, and the Leicester Angling Club had a display of specimen fish. The public house was listed as early as 1815. Tenant landlord Mr Tom Pratt is standing in the doorway.

The Duke of Rutland public house in Alfred Street, which was between Bedford Street and Fleet Street (Lee Circle). It was almost a static billboard.

The picture shown is of the Old Parliament House in Redcross Street, which later became The Inn. When Everards Brewery chose to name a new inn at Evington The Loggerheads, local residents were indignant and the name was changed to The Dove.

Yates Wine Lodge in the Market Place, c. 1982. The lodge was established in 1847. A Leicester artist painted murals on the inside walls in the 1950s.

The Blue Boar pub, from a painting. The original Blue Boar was built in 1605 and kept by Mrs Clarke. When she died it is said that her ghost haunted the place. The new Blue Boar was built in c. 1836, and closed in 1966.

The Jetty Wine Lodge, 1965, better known in days gone by as 'Page's Wine Lodge'. Mr Norman Page's grandfather took over the premises in 1825 and started a woodcarving business.

Southgate Street boasted a pub called The Chelsea Pensioner. The photograph dates from around 1900 and was taken not far from Friar Lane and the Blue Boar.

AROUND THE
STREETS

A scene in the late 1920s outside Thomas Cook's travel office in Gallowtree Gate. The car

is an 11–4 Humber saloon and is waiting for the policeman's signal to drive on.

The installation of traffic lights at the junction of St Nicholas Street and Great Central Street. The nearest set was half a mile away at the Halford Street–Rutland Street junction. Pratts Seed shop is on the right, quite a landmark in 1960.

Almost five years after the last tram, and roadworks expose the tracks in Belgrave Road, 1954.

Wharf Street in the centre of the city, part of the demolition scene in 1957.

Friday 7 June 1957 at 25A Willow Bridge Street. The home of Mr John Hollingsworth (aged 76) and his wife was in the middle of the demolition area. John and his wife eventually accepted rehousing.

Wharf Street, one of Leicester's oldest streets, looking from Bow Street towards Russell Street, 1959. The road was being widened and St Matthew's maisonettes were under construction.

A fine view of Gallowtree Gate, looking towards the Clock Tower, *c*. 1958.

Welford Road, looking from Welford Place, *c.* 1950. Campions the motorcycle shop, with manager Sid Hough, Mr BSA, is on the corner. On the right was Friswell's Cycle shop, on the corner of York Road. The Friswell Cycle was made here in the 1920s.

Gallowtree Gate, looking towards the Market Place and the Corn Exchange, 1914.

Granby Street, looking towards the Grand Hotel, *c*. 1903. Brigg's shoe shop is on the right and then Kendall's the umbrella shop.

Road works in Granby Street, 1897. The view looks towards the Midland Station. The building with the lamp on it is the Black Horse Inn.

The junction of Halford Street and Gallowtree Gate, *c.* 1938. Turner Jaques menswear shop is on the corner. Mr Jack Hill and Mr Ray Hemming, who had a menswear shop in Belvoir Street, met at Turner Jaques.

The junction of Narborough Road, Hallam Crescent East and Fullhurst Avenue, altered in 1963. The building on the right is the Roxy cinema.

SHOPS, PEOPLE, PLACES

There were three 'Knights' shops under the Grand Hotel; on the left was the clothing shop,

on the right, the shirt shop and in the middle, the middle shop for middle prices.

Photographed in 1958.

Mr K.K. Knight, the Granby Street men's outfitter, 1955. Mr Knight lived at Grey Ladies Gaulby when the author worked there in 1957. Mr George Moore, Mr Ozzie Gibson, Mr Brian Warner and Mr Roy Finn were just a few of the workmates at the time.

Hill and Hemmings menswear shop in Belvoir Street, 1955. Left to right: Mr Jack Hill, David R. Burton (the author), Mr Gordon Jones and Mr Ray Hemming.

Granby Street at the corner of York Street, 1937.

Mrs Emma French, with Peter Bradshaw, in the doorway of her corner shop at the junction of Macdonald Road and Ross Walk, Belgrave, 1925.

W. Bennett, hairdresser, newsagent and tobacconists, Humberstone Gate, 1896. Fox Lane is just off the photograph. Nearby was the Fox Hotel where Lewis's is or was. The small boy is W. Bennett junior.

The butcher's shop of W.H. Sercombe, Cavendish Road, Aylestone, *c.* 1920. The owner is second from the left and his son Henry Sercombe, aged ten, is on the right.

Elsworths the greengrocer in Wilberforce Road at the turn of the century.

The corner of Charnwood Street and Preston Street, a busy self-contained local community, 1957.

Charnwood Street or 'Charney' as the locals call it, *c.* 1957. This street was Leicester's Portobello Road. It was demolished in the early 1970s.

Cheapside was a busy place in the 1890s. The pie seller was Muggy Measures, a famous Leicester character. Wigleys store is in the background.

The staff of Vickers Mount the grocers, Gallowtree Gate, 1907. The sides of bacon outside the shop bring back tasty memories.

Lewis's in Humberstone Gate, 1990; a landmark in Leicester for many years.

Mr Mike Benson, the archivist, looks at some of Lewis's memorabilia with Ruth Hancock (left) and Debbie Glyn-Smith, 1986.

The Royal Oak at 6 Colton Street, *c.* 1890. This was a typical back street alehouse, owned by The Leicester Brewing and Malting Company. Simpkin and James storehouse was next door. Their cart, on the left of the photograph, was used to stock their famous market-place shop.

The Ginns and Gutteridge premises in Vaughan Way, 1987.

Mr William Ginns (left) and Mr Roland Jenkins drive a Victorian horse-drawn hearse through Welford Road cemetery, *c.* 1980. Mr Ginns purchased the hearse in Ireland, although it was made in Northampton by Mulliners.

Bedehouse Bathers, *c.* 1900; a cold dip even in the summer. Some of those who swam at the time are Robinson, Knight, T.R. Underwood, F. Bayliss, H. Bowers, S. Jordan, Holyoak, Daykin, Buswell and Cresswell – a very hardy bunch.

West End Adult School Dramatic Society, *c.* 1925. The production, believed to be *Mask of the Moths*, was directed by Roy and Eric Pochin.

Members of the 12th Leicester Scouts, 1929. Back row, left to right: K. Armstrong, J. Mcphee, Sid Allen (Scoutmaster), Golland senior, Revd R. Johnson, R. Mackrory, D.C. Williams (Assistant Scoutmaster), R. Woolman, Thompson, D. Butler, J. Lee. Second row: B. Salt, Warren, E. Johnson, B. Newton, A. Mckenzie, H. Moffatt, R. Biddles. Front row: W. Ratchiffe, K. Robertson, W. Flewitt, R. Garfoot, Golland junior.

The Lord Mayor of London opens Charles Street, May 1929. Beside him is Alderman Hawkes, to the left, Mr A.T. Goodman (the city surveyor) and to the right, Alderman and Mrs Wilford.

A wedding photograph of Mr Batt and Miss Ball, 17 June 1917. The photograph was taken outside the bride's parents' shop in Down Street off Melton Road. Included in the group are Staff Sergeant Lake, Police Inspector Batt, Private G. Ball, the bride and groom, Harry Batt, Mr and Mrs Ball and George Durn.

John Massey, in his distinctive woolly hat, trudged up and down the Uppingham Road for over twenty years. This photograph was taken in 1989. His favourite comment to passers-by was 'Rum weather today', and he became known as 'Rum Weather'.

The 500 unemployed Leicester men on the road to London, *c.* 1908.

A group of haymakers resting from their work in the fields which once surrounded the Wyggeston Hospital at the corner of Fosse Road South and Hinckley Road, *c.* 1910. At this time Mr Harry North, a butcher on Hinckley Road, rented the fields.

Norman and Underwood employees taking a lunch break in front of Lincoln Cathedral, which they were helping to restore, *c.* 1968. Left to right, Mr Ron Crowdwell, Mr Alec Watkin and Mr Timothy McCarthy.

David Grattan prepares to tackle the harvest with his 1938 Fordson tractor and Albion binder, *c*. 1980.

Farm workers at the city of Leicester farms on a hired traction engine which was used to drive the threshing machine, *c*. 1920.

Stableman Mr Edward Pears polishing the brasses in the tack room at the Leicester Co-op stables, *c.* 1950.

Mr Richard Vernon demonstrates steam cultivating, using engines that he owns, at the Leicestershire ploughing match, 1989. The event was organized by the *Leicester Mercury* and the Leicestershire Agricultural Society.

Mr William Blackwell, a grave digger at Gilroes cemetery, *c.* 1910. It is said that Mr Blackwell dug the very first grave when the cemetery opened *c.* 1890.

Frog Island on the River Soar, *c.* 1960. The A.E. Charlesworth factory is in the centre background.

This butcher's shop, shown *c.* 1920, was at the corner of Carlton Street. Mr Frederick Ireland, the owner, is holding the delivery bicycle. The tall girl is Frances.

Acknowledgements

As with all books, many people helped to put together this volume and without their assistance it just would not have happened. Special thanks go to my wife Beryl, son Stuart and his wife Annie, to Simon Fletcher and to Ann and Michael Potter. Finally to Steve England and his staff in the library at the *Leicester Mercury*. I thank you all most sincerely.

David R. Burton

No. 49 Charles Street, *c.* 1905. The baby is Arthur Wicks, who is being held by his grandmother. The boy with the hoop is Arthur's Uncle Tom and the aproned shopkeeper is Arthur's grandfather, a cobbler who ran the business known as Burkitts.

To order any of these titles please telephone Littlehampton Book Services on 01903 721596

ALDERNEY

Alderney: A Second Selection, *B Bonnard*

BEDFORDSHIRE

Bedfordshire at Work, *N Lutt*

BERKSHIRE

Maidenhead, *M Hayles & D Hedges*
Around Maidenhead, *M Hayles & B Hedges*
Reading, *P Southerton*
Reading: A Second Selection, *P Southerton*
Sandhurst and Crowthorne, *K Dancy*
Around Slough, *J Hunter & K Hunter*
Around Thatcham, *P Allen*
Around Windsor, *B Hedges*

BUCKINGHAMSHIRE

Buckingham and District, *R Cook*
High Wycombe, *R Goodearl*
Around Stony Stratford, *A Lambert*

CHESHIRE

Cheshire Railways, *M Hitches*
Chester, *S Nichols*

CLWYD

Clwyd Railways, *M Hitches*

CLYDESDALE

Clydesdale, *Lesmahagow Parish Historical Association*

CORNWALL

Cornish Coast, *T Bowden*
Falmouth, *P Gilson*
Lower Fal, *P Gilson*
Around Padstow, *M McCarthy*
Around Penzance, *J Holmes*
Penzance and Newlyn, *J Holmes*
Around Truro, *A Lyne*
Upper Fal, *P Gilson*

CUMBERLAND

Cockermouth and District, *J Bernard Bradbury*
Keswick and the Central Lakes, *J Marsh*
Around Penrith, *F Boyd*
Around Whitehaven, *H Fancy*

DERBYSHIRE

Derby, *D Buxton*
Around Matlock, *D Barton*

DEVON

Colyton and Seaton, *T Gosling*
Dawlish and Teignmouth, *G Gosling*
Devon Aerodromes, *K Saunders*
Exeter, *P Thomas*
Exmouth and Budleigh Salterton, *T Gosling*
From Haldon to Mid-Dartmoor, *T Hall*
Honiton and the Otter Valley, *J Yallop*
Around Kingsbridge, *K Tanner*
Around Seaton and Sidmouth, *T Gosling*
Seaton, Axminster and Lyme Regis, *T Gosling*

DORSET

Around Blandford Forum, *B Cox*
Bournemouth, *M Colman*
Bridport and the Bride Valley, *J Burrell & S Humphries*
Dorchester, *T Gosling*
Around Gillingham, *P Crocker*

DURHAM

Darlington, *G Flynn*
Darlington: A Second Selection, *G Flynn*
Durham People, *M Richardson*
Houghton-le-Spring and Hetton-le-Hole, *K Richardson*
Houghton-le-Spring and Hetton-le-Hole:
  A Second Selection, *K Richardson*
Sunderland, *S Miller & B Bell*
Teesdale, *D Coggins*
Teesdale: A Second Selection, *P Raine*
Weardale, *J Crosby*
Weardale: A Second Selection, *J Crosby*

DYFED

Aberystwyth and North Ceredigion,
  Dyfed Cultural Services Dept
Haverfordwest, *Dyfed Cultural Services Dept*
Upper Tywi Valley, *Dyfed Cultural Services Dept*

ESSEX

Around Grays, *B Evans*

GLOUCESTERSHIRE

Along the Avon from Stratford to Tewkesbury, *J Jeremiah*
Cheltenham: A Second Selection, *R Whiting*
Cheltenham at War, *P Gill*
Cirencester, *J Welsford*
Around Cirencester, *E Cuss & P Griffiths*
Forest, The, *D Mullin*
Gloucester, *J Voyce*
Around Gloucester, *A Sutton*
Gloucester: From the Walwin Collection, *J Voyce*
North Cotswolds, *D Viner*
Severn Vale, *A Sutton*
Stonehouse to Painswick, *A Sutton*
Stroud and the Five Valleys, *S Gardiner & L Padin*
Stroud and the Five Valleys: A Second Selection,
  S Gardiner & L Padin
Stroud's Golden Valley, *S Gardiner & L Padin*
Stroudwater and Thames & Severn Canals,
  E Cuss & S Gardiner
Stroudwater and Thames & Severn Canals: A Second
  Selection, *E Cuss & S Gardiner*
Tewkesbury and the Vale of Gloucester, *C Hilton*
Thornbury to Berkeley, *J Hudson*
Uley, Dursley and Cam, *A Sutton*
Wotton-under-Edge to Chipping Sodbury, *A Sutton*

GWYNEDD

Anglesey, *M Hitches*
Gwynedd Railways, *M Hitches*
Around Llandudno, *M Hitches*
Vale of Conwy, *M Hitches*

HAMPSHIRE

Gosport, *J Sadden*
Portsmouth, *P Rogers & D Francis*

HEREFORDSHIRE

Herefordshire, *A Sandford*

HERTFORDSHIRE

Barnet, *I Norrie*
Hitchin, *A Fleck*
St Albans, *S Mullins*
Stevenage, *M Appleton*

ISLE OF MAN

The Tourist Trophy, *B Snelling*

ISLE OF WIGHT

Newport, *D Parr*
Around Ryde, *D Parr*

JERSEY

Jersey: A Third Selection, *R Lemprière*

KENT

Bexley, *M Scott*
Broadstairs and St Peter's, *J Whyman*
Bromley, Keston and Hayes, *M Scott*
Canterbury: A Second Selection, *D Butler*
Chatham and Gillingham, *P MacDougall*
Chatham Dockyard, *P MacDougall*
Deal, *J Broady*
Early Broadstairs and St Peter's, *B Wootton*
East Kent at War, *D Collyer*
Eltham, *J Kennett*
Folkestone: A Second Selection, *A Taylor & E Rooney*
Goudhurst to Tenterden, *A Guilmant*
Gravesend, *R Hiscock*
Around Gravesham, *R Hiscock & D Grierson*
Herne Bay, *J Hawkins*
Lympne Airport, *D Collyer*
Maidstone, *I Hales*
Margate, *R Clements*
RAF Hawkinge, *R Humphreys*
RAF Manston, *RAF Manston History Club*
RAF Manston: A Second Selection,
  RAF Manston History Club
Ramsgate and Thanet Life, *D Perkins*
Romney Marsh, *E Carpenter*
Sandwich, *C Wanostrocht*
Around Tonbridge, *C Bell*
Tunbridge Wells, *M Rowlands & I Beavis*
Tunbridge Wells: A Second Selection,
  M Rowlands & I Beavis
Around Whitstable, *C Court*
Wingham, Adisham and Littlebourne, *M Crane*

LANCASHIRE

Around Barrow-in-Furness, *J Garbutt & J Marsh*
Blackpool, *C Rothwell*
Bury, *J Hudson*
Chorley and District, *J Smith*
Fleetwood, *C Rothwell*
Heywood, *J Hudson*
Around Kirkham, *C Rothwell*
Lancashire North of the Sands, *J Garbutt & J Marsh*
Around Lancaster, *S Ashworth*
Lytham St Anne's, *C Rothwell*
North Fylde, *C Rothwell*
Radcliffe, *J Hudson*
Rossendale, *B Moore & N Dunnachie*

LEICESTERSHIRE

Around Ashby-de-la-Zouch, *K Hillier*
Charnwood Forest, *I Keil, W Humphrey & D Wix*
Leicester, *D Burton*
Leicester: A Second Selection, *D Burton*
Melton Mowbray, *T Hickman*
Around Melton Mowbray, *T Hickman*
River Soar, *D Wix, P Shacklock & I Keil*
Rutland, *T Clough*
Vale of Belvoir, *T Hickman*
Around the Welland Valley, *S Mastoris*

LINCOLNSHIRE

Grimsby, *J Tierney*
Around Grimsby, *J Tierney*
Grimsby Docks, *J Tierney*
Lincoln, *D Cuppleditch*